- Book 4 -

Shadow and Friends

European Vacation

by

S. Jackson,

A. Raymond, & M. Schmidt

READERS' FAVORITE®
FIVE STARS

Copyright

Shadow and Friends European Vacation

In Shadow and Friends European Vacation, a small dog named Shadow wins a free trip to Europe because of all her books that teach children safety at home, and during adventures. Shadow is allowed five friends with her on this fabulous trip, and she chooses to take five squirrel friends. In this delightful and funny book for children, safety is taught through the hilarious antics of her friends. Throughout this story of teaching children about historical areas and places in Europe, squirrel antics keep children entertained, and safety is learned. Targeted at ages 4-11, this book is easy to read and perfect for home or classroom. This story illustrates a few of Europe's fascinating features with illustrations for children and adults.

All text copyright © S. Jackson, A. Raymond, & M. Schmidt
Cover design by S. Jackson, A. Raymond, & M. Schmidt
Interior design © S. Jackson, A. Raymond, & M. Schmidt

Print history
First edition published March 2016

ISBN-13: 978-0-692-17621-4 (S. Jackson, A. Raymond, M. Schmidt, G. Donley)
ISBN-10: 978-0-692-17620-7

Library of Congress Cataloguing-in-Publication Data

SHADOW AND FRIENDS
EUROPEAN VACATION

By

S. Jackson, A. Raymond
&
M. Schmidt

Reviews

"Shadow and Friends European Vacation" is a cute and hilarious book for those with children of all ages, and certainly hits age target range of 4–11. I laughed right along with my grandchildren as I read this funny story to them. No one would ever expect to see a squirrel zip-line down from the observation deck of the Eiffel tower, let alone four squirrels! Shadow certainly taught the squirrels and children about safety after that escapade, amid lots of laughter. Jackson managed to keep this learning story fun while teaching at the same time and keeping my grandchildren captivated throughout. This book is perfect for home, schools, and libraries. I highly recommend this book.
~ Susan Vance, Author, "Leaving Savannah."

This is a wonderful book to entertain and teach children about safety. Using a dog and squirrels that traveled was very creative and it showed the importance of being careful while having fun. I rated this book a 5 Star for kids 4 to 10.
~ Raven H. Price, Author, "Convinced."

Dedication

Always to Eli, Joshua, Noah, and Rachel who taught us so much
about life on Earth;
To the sweetest baby boy, our grandson, Austin;
To the sweetest little baby girl, our granddaughter, Emma;
Always to Michael, my beloved husband, partner, and best friend
in the entire world;
Always to Mary, my beloved wife, partner, and best friend in the
entire world;
We are true soul-mates.

Shadow, a small dog, woke up excited this morning. Yesterday she was informed that she won an all expense paid trip to Europe! Shadow barked softly in excitement!

ruff bark

bark bark

Shadow won the trip because of her books, that teach children safety at home, and during adventures. Shadow could take five friends with her!

Listen to grownups

Stay safe

Look before crossing the street

Ask for help when lost

Don't bully others

After breakfast, she went to visit and invite her squirrel friends, Uncle Stubby, Foxy, Big Whitey, Little Whitey, and Pilot Squirrel to go with her. They all said YES!

Once packed, they hopped inside the Rodent Road Adventure Tours jet and Pilot flew the jet airplane! He sure could fly! He could fly, drive a car, and he knew travel safety. All of the squirrels thought Pilot was smart!!

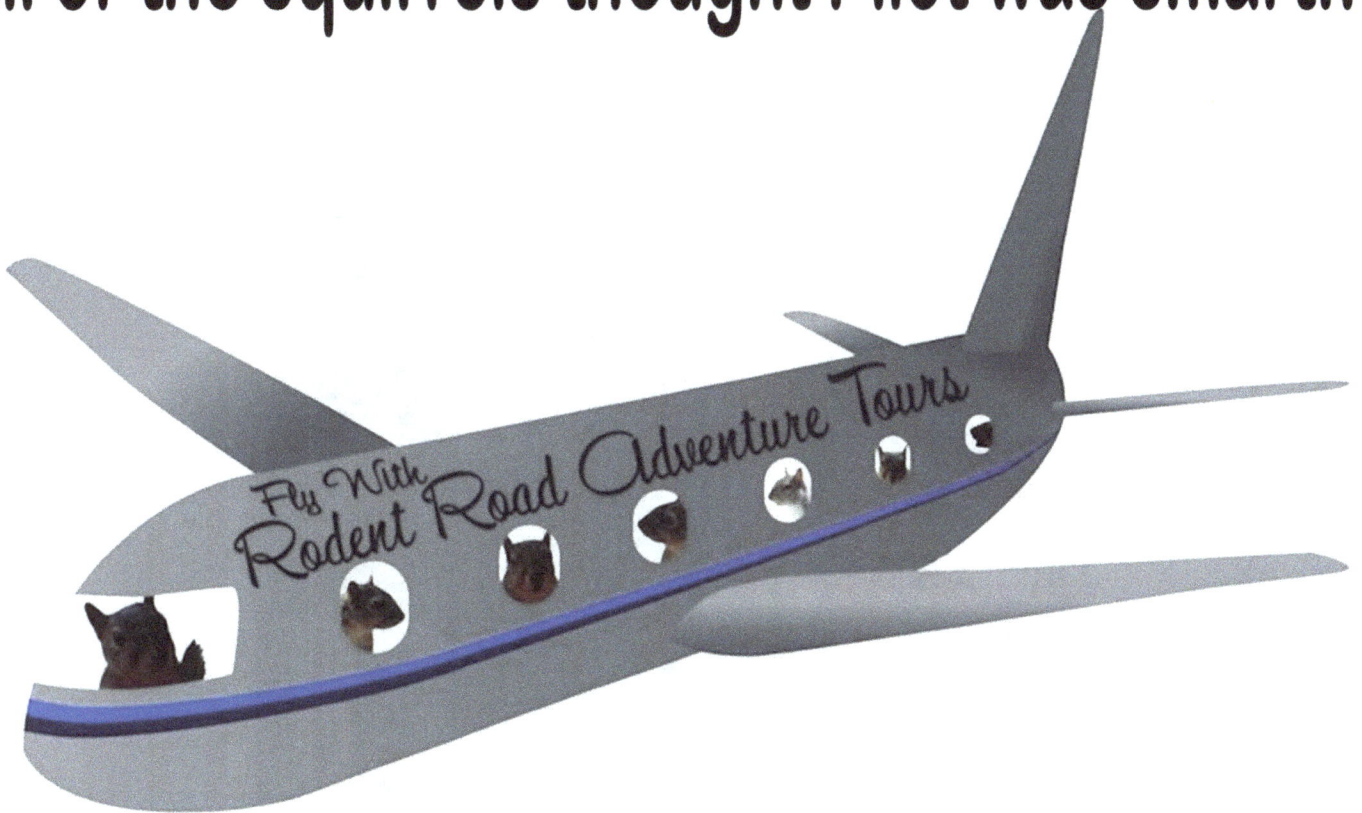

After landing at Heathrow Airport, London, England, Shadow and Little Whitey jumped on the top of a red double-decker bus! Pilot said, "Get down from there! To be safe, we must ride inside the bus."

The bus dropped them off at the Tower of London. Foxy wanted to see the Crown Jewels and the Queen's coronation gown. While looking at necklaces, Foxy disappeared. Where did she go? Then they saw her!

Foxy had dressed up in the Queen's coronation gown and she was wearing the coronation crown!!! The curator at the Tower said, "Foxy! You must take the gown and jewelry off right now!"

Foxy did what he said, and they all learned that the gown and jewels were for display only. The curator told them that the coronation crown is used for each king or queen when it is their turn to be crowned!

"Let's go see Big Ben!" Shouted Little Whitey. Pilot rented a car and drove them to see Big Ben, a huge square clock near the top of a tower! They listened to the clock chimes while they ate their snacks.

Uncle Stubby said, "I would like to go see Stonehenge. Cousin Red lives near there, and it will be a nice place to stay for the night." Pilot drove them to Stonehenge, a huge old monument.

At Stonehenge, they learned that the stones were old, and that they were called 'trilithons'. A trilithon is two large vertical stones with a third stone set horizontally across the top.

Not far from Stonehenge, and in a forest of pine trees, they found the home of Cousin Red. Red got his name because he comes from the family of Eurasia red squirrels. Red was a tree squirrel, too.

Red was happy to see his cousins and Shadow! He invited them to dinner, and to stay the night inside his squirrel nest in the pine trees. Shadow ate dog food and slept in her special doggie bed.

The next morning, they said goodbye, and climbed back inside the car. Big Whitey wanted to go to Paris, and he wanted to see the Eiffel Tower! After arriving in Paris, they decided to eat before going to the Eiffel Tower.

They took the elevator up to the observation deck of the Eiffel Tower. They could see for miles! "I brought a zip line." Big Whitey said, and before anyone could stop him, he ZIPPED all the way back down to the ground!

"Here I come, Daddy!" Little Whitey yelled, and just as fast as his dad, he ZIPPED down to the ground! Foxy was afraid they would get into trouble, and just then Uncle Stubby and Pilot ZIPPED down the line!!

Only Foxy and Shadow were left on the observation deck of the Eiffel Tower! Foxy cut the zip line from the tower, and they took the elevator back down to the ground. The others were waiting for them.

Shadow said, "You must all behave on the rest of this trip or we are flying back home now!" The five squirrels agreed to behave and they set out for the Louvre. The Louvre is the world's largest museum, and a historic monument in Paris!

Foxy wanted to see the Mona Lisa, a painting of a woman by the famous Italian artist, Leonardo da Vinci. Foxy just had to see the most famous painting in the whole world, and so they did just that!

Foxy asked if they could visit Neuschwanstein Castle in Germany next. All of them decided the castle looked grand. They learned that Disneyland's Sleeping Beauty Castle was inspired by this castle!

After eating nuts and dog food, Shadow and the squirrels found a spot to rest for the night near the castle. Shadow set up her doggie bed, and they all fell asleep quite fast!

The next morning, they set out early for Italy. Their first stop was the Leaning Tower of Pisa. No one knows for sure who started building the famous tower, and it is safe to visit.

After lunch, they set out for Rome and the famous Colosseum! Shadow and her friends took a lot of 'selfies' in front of the Colosseum. The Colosseum was old, and built of concrete and sand!

After walking and running all over the Colosseum, they became tired, and Uncle Stubby found a nice shady old tree to rest under. They chose to eat and then they settled down in a safe spot for the night.

When morning came, they set off for Vatican City. Everyone wanted to see St. Peter's Basilica, the museums, and Sistine Chapel. They were amazed at the beautiful frescoes painted by Michelangelo, and they took pictures!

After dinner, they found a safe area to sleep for the night, but Shadow and her squirrel friends were sad. This was the last night of their European vacation.

They saw Uncle Stubby's twin near the top of the Empire State Building on their flight back to Kansas!! They made their way home, and everyone was tired and happy to be home once again.

Author Bio

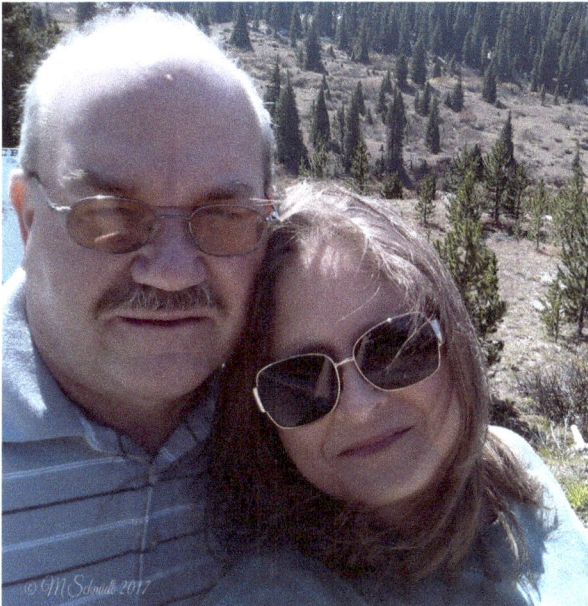

S. Jackson is a retired registered nurse; a member of the Catholic Church, and has taught kindergarten Catechism; she has worked in various capacities for The American Cancer Society, March of Dimes, Cub and Boy Scouts, (son, Noah, is an Eagle Scout), and sponsored trips for high school children music. She loves all forms of art but mostly focuses on the visual arts; such as amateur photography, traditional, and graphic art as her health allows.

A. Raymond is a member of the Catholic Church, and has helped his wife with The American Cancer Society, March of Dimes, Cub and Boy Scouts, and sponsored children alongside his wife on music trips. He devotes his spare time to fishing, reading, playing poker, Jeeping, and travel adventures with his wife. Both love spending time with their grandson, Austin, and granddaughter Emma.

www.ingramcontent.com/pod-product-compliance
Lightning Source LLC
Chambersburg PA
CBHW062022090426
42811CB00005B/926